FATHER – GERALD

SISTER – CHARIS

JAMES WRIFFLE MP
CHARIS'S HUSBAND

ARTHUR

BABY PATRICIA

A Victorian
Cat's Journal

A Victorian Cat's Journal

30 paintings by
SUSAN HERBERT
Text by
STANLEY BARON

A Bulfinch Press Book
Little, Brown and Company
Boston • Toronto • London

Monday 15th

*T*he early afternoon was so fresh and temperate that my three darlings and I spent over an hour in the park. We strolled up and down the paths together, admiring the many beds of varied flowers until we were a mite tired. Then sister Letitia came to meet us with a huge fur rug which we spread over one of the public benches before sitting down to restore ourselves.

Friday 10th

*T*omorrow we will be having our last formal dinner party of the season and Mrs Goodstone is already deep in preparations. There will be eight at table, and we have taken great pains over the menu. Mrs Goodstone, as is her habit, listens to my suggestions with apparent interest, but then tells me exactly what she wishes to cook. I thereupon have to counter with other alternatives, and we bargain back and forth like traders in a Levantine souk. I believe, in truth, that Mrs Goodstone prevails more often than I do, but I recognize that the main consideration is that she must be kept in good humour until the last course is served.

Saturday 11th

I feel quite confident that last evening's dinner party was, after all, quite a success. The table decorations were most attractive, and everyone seemed to enjoy all seven courses that emerged from Mrs Goodstone's kitchen. The wines were much savoured, particularly by Gerald who had selected them with care. Conversation was uninterrupted, and I detected no awkward moments at all.

I was slightly apprehensive beforehand about Lady Maddingly, whom I had never entertained before, but she was so warm and unaffected that my fears were soon allayed. I admired her delicate diamond tiara, and she was most flattering in her attentions to both me and Gerald. It was a shame that Lord Maddingly should have keeled over as he tried to stand up from the table when the menfolk prepared to join the women, but fortunately he suffered no injury at all. In fact, he asked at once for another glass of port.

Wednesday 15th

*L*etitia is such a help to me! She seems to be quite happy carrying out tedious little errands on my behalf, such as buying a length of pink ribbon at Mrs Wishall's millinery shop. While Letitia was there earlier today concentrating on choosing the correct colour, I'm afraid that our little terror Arthur frightened his dear sister by pulling her hair. What was even worse, he contrived to make a mess of one spool of ribbon while no one was keeping an eye on him. Mrs Wishall might seek to keep her wares out of Master Arthur's reach another time.

Susan L. Herbert

Saturday 25th

My visits to the greenhouse are not very serious. They are prompted by my wish to make the gardener aware that I do occasionally inspect the results of his work, though the churlish man has proven on the whole to be fairly reliable.

Today I found most of the plants looking a bit starved; the fuchsia and geraniums looked to me unusually leggy and a trifle neglected. I had to tie up one pot of lilies which were in grave danger of overbalancing.

Arthur is quite endearing in the greenhouse. He pretends to be repotting some nameless plant, and all he does is to cover himself with loose dirt until he looks like a Moor.

Thursday 30th

A game of whist often helps to while away the afternoon hours. Ever since our neighbour Abigail Root has been widowed, she invites me to participate in her card games, but I usually find myself with so little time to spare that I have to decline. Yesterday, however, I felt compelled to accept her invitation and so I passed some two or more agreeable hours in her company and that of her great friend Mrs Mitchell-Fielding, who is a well-informed and lively person, though slightly pretentious about her connections with the Royal Family. Slight is indeed what they are!

Tuesday 4th

How true is the phrase: time flies! I could hardly believe the evidence of my own eyes this afternoon when I saw our Arthur actually perched on a two-wheeled bicycle, trying manfully to stay mounted on the wretched thing with the help of his devoted sisters. It brought a gentle tear to my eye to consider that Arthur was a wee helpless infant only a few years ago. Now he is a fearless, growing boy. I had to stop myself from rushing out of doors and lifting him off of the odious contraption, as I instinctively wished to do. But I had to let my little boy take his chances without my interference.

Thursday 6th

We have had to hire a new upstairs maid because the last one, ungrateful Prentice, departed suddenly and with no explanation at all two weeks ago. Letitia interviewed some ten girls before she chose Carrie, who had previously been employed in the home of Lady Murdstone. Carrie appears to be neat and willing and respectful, but her expression does seem to me sullen. Ah me, how deplorable I find domestic problems!

Saturday 8th

*F*rom time to time, Gerald will indulge me in a musical evening at home. I have not a great deal of talent, to be sure, but I find it most relaxing to play certain of my favourite compositions at the pianoforte. Georgina has shown a certain aptitude for the violin and Nannie has been accompanying her to Madame Vetrinelli for lessons once every fortnight, but the dear girl does not seem to be making noticeable progress.

Saturday 15th

*W*hat can be more delightful than a summer's day tea-party in a formal garden? As we were visited yesterday by Cousin Alberta and her three grown children, we took the opportunity to set out in three carriages in order to see the famous gardens of Locksmythe Castle. It was one of those perfect early summer days with scarcely a breeze to disturb our coiffures. The tea was delicious and served with excellent cakes (of which Arthur had far too many!).

I thought that Cousin Alberta and her daughter Harriet were rather dowdy in their attire. Both of her unfortunate sons were exceeding dull!

*T*oday we celebrate fifty glorious years of our dear Queen's reign, and we do so with pride and fervour. Who could not but admire the fortitude and grace with which our beloved monarch has accepted her exalted role in life and all the burdens that go with it! When I think of Her Majesty's overwhelming responsibilities, I am ashamed that I ever find it in myself to complain of the petty problems in my daily round! God save the Queen!

Friday 5th

*G*erald's sister has disgraced the family! I have always felt secretly that Charis was a flighty, excessively romantic young woman, though I have never expressed this to Gerald. Once she had married James Wriffle M.P., everyone sighed with relief, though I continued to look on her as a frivolous goose whose head could easily be turned.

And now, alas, I have been proven right! It appears - and I blush to write this - that she has been having a liaison for several months with dear James's <u>closest friend</u>, a man we all <u>knew</u> and <u>trusted</u>, Percival Pringle. I could hardly believe my ears yesterday evening when Gerald told me, in his gravest voice, that Charis and Percival have eloped! I have taken to my bed, for I cannot face my relatives and friends who will be driving up to the house to offer me their condolences.

One can only be grateful that our tragic Charis leaves no innocent babes behind her. Oh, how we are tried!

Saturday 13th

*G*erald is in a most happy frame of mind now that the cricket season is upon us again. I know few women who find any pleasure in this curious sport; certainly I do not. Gerald, however, is ever hopeful and does his best to explain the fine points of cricket to me. It is quite hopeless. I still cannot understand the difference between a yorker and silly mid-off, or whether a century or a duck is something good or bad. Every now and then I venture to say, "Well played!" but I do so only after I see that Gerald is unusually aroused by some activity on what he calls the pitch.

Saturday 20th

*M*y dashing young brother Handley came to call late this morning, and regaled me with tales of his latest social activities. The handsome boy is much in demand, and seems to have been pursued most recently by one family in particular, the Fairbrothers, who have a marriageable daughter. Handley described in detail a pique-nique he attended not long ago on the Fairbrothers' estate, where the young people indulged in some light-hearted flirtation between cups of tea. Handley maintained that the company was boring beyond words and that young Miss F., though rich, is indescribably plain.

Monday 22nd

I was reminded yesterday by a visit from my old school chum Matilda Gliff of the time she and I travelled together to Switzerland. Our chaperone throughout the journey was Matilda's former Nannie, Granger, who never let us out of her sight except when we were asleep. Matilda surprised me by recalling that we wore identical travelling costumes and were determined to imitate each other in everything we did. Fancy! What foolish young girls we were! And yet how we did enjoy ourselves!

Saturday 10th

I know that nowadays seaside resorts are meant to be healthful for all of us, and particularly salutary for young children, but I am bound to say that I find no great pleasure in them myself. Therefore, I was not at all reluctant to permit sister Letitia and Nannie to take the children off for five days last week to Margate Sands. My little ones were evidently quick to make friends with other children on the beach. Nannie tells me that Arthur showed his usual tendency to misbehave, but that Baby Patricia was, as always, an angel.

I must say that Letitia has returned from this outing in an unfamiliar glow. I cannot but wonder whether she has met an interesting gentleman, but dare not ask her outright.

Wednesday 21st

*S*ince Monday we have been visiting Scotland. The lodge we have taken for three weeks is not far from our dear Queen's beloved Balmoral, amid varied scenery of the most beautiful kind imaginable. It tempts me to bring out my neglected watercolours and try to capture some of the wondrous sights of the area. How easily I am affected by Nature in all her grandeur!

The area is renowned for its golf links and all day long we are able to observe gentlemen in suitable golfing garb exercising their skills (or indeed their lack of them) with the clubs. Gerald admits that he would not be averse to seeing whether he has an aptitude for this exercise, but he is fearful lest he subject himself to the ridicule of those who are more proficient.

susan L Herbert

Nannie spent a part of the day as usual in the park though she let it be known afterwards that there was "a proper autumn nip" in the air. Dear Nannie will complain whatever the weather! Only last week she was grumbling over what she called the hottest summer she could remember! It is true that I find her a trial sometimes, but she is so reliable as far as Baby Patricia is concerned and lifts that responsibility off my shoulders. Arthur and Felicity seem to be quite fond of Nannie, even though she is occasionally severe with them, and look forward to visiting the park in her company.

Sunday 22nd

I am sorry to have to admit that Arthur can be a truly naughty boy! Today I was in the orchard with him and Georgina and Felicity. I was daydreaming while rocking Felicity gently in the swing when I happened quite by chance to notice that Arthur was endeavouring to untie one of the ropes that secure the swing to a branch of the tree. What a shock it caused me! I dare not think what might have ensued if the hand of God had not led me to detect Arthur's wickedness in time! I feel quite faint when I think how close poor Felicity came to tumbling to the ground and perhaps even breaking one of her tender limbs! Arthur has been sent to bed without his supper, and I will have to discuss this seriously with his father.

Tuesday 8th

*C*ousin Archibald and his dear wife Sophia did Gerald and me the great honour of inviting us to be their guests at the Opera. I was, of course, delighted, as I am extremely fond of music in general and the operatic form in particular. Gerald is less enthusiastic than I, and so I was not entirely surprised when he discovered at a late hour that his presence would be required that very evening in Newcastle-upon-Tyne. With some trepidation I suggested to Sophia that I might bring Arthur in Gerald's stead, and was happy to hear her say that she thought it a splendid idea.

Arthur was quite excited at first by the grand people in the audience, the splendour of the historical theatre, and the special privilege of sitting in a private box; but the poor little lad drifted into sleep soon after the curtain rose. I fear he is more like Gerald than me where music is concerned. The opera was one of my favourites, *Lucia di Lammermoor,* and though I do not know who sang the parts of Lucy and Edgar, or whether they sang well, I found the whole evening most enjoyable.

During this inclement weather, several of my friends in the neighbourhood have joined me in evening embroidery sessions, which we all enjoy thoroughly. Snug in one corner of our well-heated morning room, we do some fine needlework together and also have the opportunity to discuss various entertaining or disturbing aspects of our community, such as the recent arrival of the new vicar and his haughty wife, the Millingtons' cook who appears to have eloped with the Winslows' butler (a married man, to be sure), and other events of similar general interest.

Tuesday 22nd

*H*aving heard for many years that music halls were wicked places, I recently asked Handley if he had ever attended one. Oh yes, indeed! he said. (I could see that he wanted to be looked upon as a man of the world in spite of his tender age.)

He remarked, to my surprise, that what one saw on the stage of a musical hall was rarely wicked and rarely entertaining. Apart from a handful of artistes who had a real talent to make one laugh or to enthrall one with their singing, most of the performers, Handley said, were rather pitiful. I could not refrain from laughing as he described a pair of elderly women canaries (as he called them), often under the influence of gin, who are known as "The Siamese Twins" and sing a song that goes: "Oh how I love Siam, From there is where I am, My name is Ko-mai-tin, And I'm a Siamese twin . . ."

*O*n Monday last the Riverdales gave one of the most splendid balls of the season in their sumptuous mansion in Kensington. Since I have been acquainted with Dorothea Riverdale from the time when she was merely Miss Dorothea Webb and a slip of a girl, Gerald and I were naturally invited to partake of the evening's pleasures. We arrived at the fashionable hour of twenty past 10 to find the grand house, which is full of precious objects and expensive furnishings, crowded with fashionable people, the bon ton indeed! I recognized one extravagant Worth ball gown, all in pink with many ruffles, and Gerald was pleased to encounter two City gentlemen who belong to one of his Clubs.

The dear children were in the midst of their geography lesson when the snow began to fall today. Miss Wilhelmina Leverstoke, who instructs the boys in maths and spelling, as well as geography, was thoughtful enough to tell sister Letitia that our Arthur is one of her best-behaved and attentive boys. This was certainly surprising in view of his sometimes unruly conduct at home, but all the same he was permitted an extra Bakewell tart with his tea, though I refrained from telling him what he owed this treat to, for fear of turning his head. I do hope that Letitia, who is inclined to be slightly indulgent towards her nephew, followed my example.

I have been poorly for two days now, but our good Doctor Wainscott assures me it is only a mild grippe and that it will pass by the end of the week. Aunt Drummond came to call and to see if there was anything she could do to help. Aunt is always on hand when someone is ill or in difficulties - such thoughtfulness! Alas, I was feeling so miserable and infirm that I fear I did not properly express my appreciation. Aunt Drummond is such a sensitive soul that I must not neglect to write her a note as soon as ever I am recovered.

*T*he cold weather has truly settled in, and it was still snowing tonight when we returned home from Evensong. There are several inches of snow already on the ground and no one can say when this downfall will stop.

The girls were all dressed warmly and appreciated their little fur collars. I have a new fur muff for the season and will surely get a good deal of use out of it.

*L*etitia and Mr Hawksborough were skating on the ice-covered pond this early evening after tea. Mr Hawksborough, whom Letitia learned to know during the summer at Margate Sands, has been showering the dear girl with affectionate attentions and gifts, and makes little secret of his hopes. Gerald hears nothing but good reports of the young gentleman, whose people have a seat in Bedfordshire, so I am hopeful that we may soon hear the happy news.

Christmas Eve was as happy an occasion as I can remember. Thanks to the dear Lord, our whole family were in good health, Arthur having recovered over the weekend from his dreadful croup, and we were all in a very merry disposition. Though we do keep in mind the seriousness of what we celebrate at this time of year and try to keep the frivolity to a minimum.

The children adored the tree which I had helped to decorate the evening before, and of course they are as always agog to learn what presents they will receive on Christmas morn.

Friday 15th

I am delighted to record that Letitia's wedding was a dignified and moving event. Mr Hawksborough's family were as gracious as one might have expected, and our own relations, numerous and widespread though they may be, all graced the solemn occasion with their presence.

Dearest Letitia was naturally apprehensive beforehand, and I detected a furtive tear in her eye while she was being dressed. But once the ceremony began - and I must say that our new vicar, Mr Bycroft, conducted it admirably - everything went smoothly indeed. The reception and the food prepared for it by Cook Goodstone were much enjoyed by everyone.

Monday 25th

It has been my fondest hope for years to hang my father's portrait in the library, but I did not achieve that aim until yesterday morning when Mother finally relinquished it to me. Posed by his favourite falls in his beloved Highlands and carrying his favourite walking-stick, my dear dear father is finally restored to me as I remember him best - upright, thoughtful and dignified.

First United States Edition

Library of Congress Cataloging-in-Publication Data

Herbert, Susan, 1945-
  A Victorian Cat's Journal : 30 paintings / by Susan Herbert; text
by Stanley Baron. — 1st U.S. ed.
      p.   cm.
  "A Bulfinch Press Book."
  ISBN 0–8212–1865–4
  1. Herbert, Susan, 1945–   . 2. Cats in art. I. Baron, Stanley.
II. Title.
  ND497.H49A4   1991
  759.2 — dc20   91-2353

Bulfinch Press is an imprint and trademark of
Little, Brown and Company (Inc.)
Published simultaneously in Canada by Little, Brown & Company
(Canada) Limited

PRINTED IN HONG KONG